CHILD
SEXUAL
ABUSE

Thinking Biblically about the Unthinkable

By Cheryl Bell

Association of Certified
Biblical Counselors

As we face the issues of sin and suffering in a broken world, we all need wisdom from God. Thankfully, the Lord has given us all that we need for life and godliness through His sufficient Word (2 Peter 1:3; 2 Timothy 3:16).

ACBC's Truth in Love resources are designed to bring the rich truth of God's character and promises to bear on the problems people face in everyday life. As you walk with others, seeking to minister the very words of God to them, we pray this booklet will be a resource that points you back to His truth and equips you to admonish the idle, encourage the fainthearted, and help the weak (1 Thessalonians 5:14).

Author

Cheryl Bell is an Adjunct Professor of Biblical Counseling and Women's Studies at Southwestern Baptist Theological Seminary and an Adjunct Professor of Biblical Counseling at Midwestern Baptist Theological Seminary.

Child sexual abuse is a difficult topic to address, not because the facts are unknown but because it is a topic we would rather not have to face. There is no pleasant way to describe an adult's misuse of authority or physical strength to satisfy his or her sexual desires at the expense of a child.

You may be unaware of the types of acts that are classified as sexual abuse, and it is important to recognize that the scope of these activities can be broad. This type of abuse includes "fondling, lewd or lascivious exposure or behavior, intercourse, sodomy, oral copulation, penetration of a genital or anal opening by a foreign object, child pornography, child prostitution, and any other 'sexual conduct harmful to a child's mental, emotional, or physical welfare.' These acts may be forced upon the child or the child may be coaxed, seduced, and persuaded to cooperate. The absence of force or coercion does not diminish the abusive nature of the conduct, but, sadly, it may cause the child to feel responsible for what has occurred."[1] Acts that meet these qualifications are clearly within the realm of child sexual abuse from a legal perspective and must be reported to legal authorities.

---

[1] Ken Paxton, Attorney General of Texas, "What Can We Do About Child Abuse?" Accessed January 23, 2017, https://www.texasattorneygeneral.gov/cvs/what-we-can-do-about-child-abuse-1#sexual.

Ultimately, God and His dictates supersede any human codes. Scripture is clear in its expression of God's love for children and His wrath against those who mistreat them (Matthew 18:1-14). Believers must respond to this great wrong by the means God has provided. We do this by comforting and counseling the abused and turning over the abuser to legal authorities to suffer the consequences of his or her choices.[2]

Research demonstrates that child sexual abuse occurs more frequently with girls than with boys, and 90 percent of offenders are men. Victimization by a stranger is uncommon, and 90 percent of victims are abused by someone they know and trust.[3]

Researchers agree that at least one-fourth of all girls have experienced some measure of sexual abuse, and at least one-third of girls with this traumatic history suffer from significant after-effects into adulthood. The statistics on the sexual

---

[2] For information on reporting within your state see: www.rainn.org.

[3] Greg Love, "Safeguarding Church Ministry Conference," lecture presented on behalf of the Southern Baptist Convention of Texas, North Richland Hills, TX, March 31, 2016.

abuse of boys tell us that one in six boys have been abused as well.[4]

Reportedly 66 percent of abused children do not speak of their abuse until many years after it has occurred.[5] This silence is often due to the extreme nature of the trauma and the negative responses associated with the initial abuse.

Long-Term Effects

Child sexual abuse is a traumatic experience that may contribute to a number of long-term after-effects. While the trauma does not predict that a person will experience long-term effects, there is certainly a correlation of symptoms that may include one or more of the following: anxiety, depression, guilt and shame, anger, unforgiveness, bitterness, distrust, interpersonal relationship issues, self-destructive behaviors, and sexual problems. Victims of child sexual abuse may exhibit a variety of these side effects and therefore can struggle in a variety of ways. These cases can be difficult to counsel and the counselor must be dependent on the Holy Spirit and Scripture in order to address the variety of heart issues and outward

[4] Love, "Safeguarding Church Ministry Conference."

[5] Ibid.

behavioral manifestations in a counselee who has experienced this kind of abuse.

In child sexual abuse, the sins of another are what lie at the heart of the suffering that victims experience. The powerlessness and innocence of the child makes him or her vulnerable to sexual abuse simply because he or she is a child. The sadness and grief in the abused child's heart that result from these abusive experiences are a normal response and not sinful in any way. Despite the depth of such emotion, children abused in this way most often attempt to hide these feelings. If the abuse is discovered, weeping with those who weep is a proper response from Christ's body, the church (Romans 12:15). In the aftermath of child sexual abuse, the abused child or adult can be comforted as each comes to understand his or her suffering from God's perspective. God's ability to use it for good in making them like Christ is not limited by anything—even the extreme nature of the assault against them (Romans 8:28-29).

Yet, in many cases, the cause of a victim's suffering is more complicated. The abused child may add to his or her own pain with a sinful response to the offense and toward the offender. This begins as she turns away from God or even assigns blame to Him in anger and bitterness, knowing that He could have prevented her abuse. As a consequence, the child follows the abuser's example, as both of them are ruled by sinful desires, thoughts, and behaviors.

In making this choice, the child has followed his or her abuser's lead and turned to sin rather than to God. The child's sinful behavior may not look the same as that of her abuser, but her choice to reject God does demonstrate that abuser's power over her. The only way for the child to resist her abuser's power is to submit to God and obey His command to forgive her abuser (Matthew 6:12, 14-15; 18:21-22; 5:43-48; Luke 6:27; 1 Peter 2:21-23).

It is important to note that forgiveness does not equate to the restoration of the relationship, because apart from salvation and transformation in the life of the abuser, the danger to the child remains. In fact, the abuser must be reported to the legal authorities and prosecuted for this criminal offense.

In cases of child sexual abuse, children suffer because they have been sinned against. We must focus on helping them respond biblically to the dark offenses committed against them that contribute to their suffering. Additionally, counselors must also recognize that child may be suffering as a result of sinning in response to their abuse. One of the most difficult topics to address is the sinful response of the abused child to his or her abuser, and yet these wrong responses contribute to the long-term after-effects of child sexual abuse. Research has suggested that it is not the abuse itself that produces the long-term negative outcomes, but rather the way in which the child thinks about the abuse that either produces or prevents those outcomes.[6] Therefore, we must address the heart of the abused individual in order to prevent long-term after-effects in sexually abused children and to resolve the existing long-term after-effects in adult survivors.

---

[6] Sabina Arin and Susan Nolen-Hoeksema, "The Dangers of Dwelling: An Examination of the Relationship Between Rumination and Consumptive Coping in Survivors of Childhood Sexual Abuse," *Cognition and Emotion* 24, no. 1 (2010): 71-85; Terry Lynn Gall, Viola Basque, Marizette Damasceno-Scott, and Gerard Vardy, "Spirituality and the Current Adjustment of Adult Survivors of Childhood Sexual Abuse," *Journal for the Scientific Study of Religion,* 46 no. 1 (2007): 101-117; and Claire Marriott, Catherine Hamilton-Giachritisis, and Chris Harrop, "Factors Promoting Resilience Following Childhood Sexual Abuse: A Structured, Narrative Review of the Literature," *Child Abuse Review* 23 (2014): 17-34.

God's Truth About Child Sexual Abuse

Someone who has been sexually abused as a child may respond to their abuse in one or more of the following common ways. In each case, it is our responsibility as biblical counselors to point them to the truth found in God's Word that addresses their response. Since one or more of these responses to abuse are common, this knowledge is useful in formulating and asking counselees good questions.

Anxiety

Anxiety is a topic addressed by God in His Word. He describes these fears as burdens (Psalm 55:22), troubled hearts (John 14:27), anxious thoughts (Psalm 139:23-24), and worries about life (Matthew 6:25; Luke 10:38-42). According to Psalm 139:23-24, these anxious thoughts are a component of the heart that God examines. These thoughts are powerful, for they produce self-inflicted wounds that are the distinguishing marks of anxiety.

Thankfully, God does not simply describe anxiety. In Philippians 4:6-9, He prescribes a remedy. For the believer who accepts God's remedy, prayer with thanksgiving brings the resolution that replaces anxiety with peace. An ongoing discipline of the mind that replaces anxious thoughts with God's truths ensures that the very heart and mind that entertained those anxious thoughts are now guarded by His peace.

These simple biblical truths can be taught to women with long-term effects as well as to children who report abuse. The biblical response prescribed in Philippians 4:6-9 is simple enough for a child to obey.

Depression

While depression is a word that may not be found in Scripture, there are many biblical synonyms. The biblical text uses words like "distress" (1 Samuel 30:6), "downcast" (2 Corinthians 7:5-7 ESV), "dismayed" (Deuteronomy 31:8), and "brokenhearted" (Psalm 34:18) to depict depression. Scripture both describes and prescribes remedies for these conditions.

In cases of child sexual abuse, it is important to distinguish between the justified sorrow that comes from victimization and sinful depression. Depression is often the result of a wrong response to a difficult situation, and yet, difficult situations are incapable of producing depression. The child who sorrows in response to child sexual abuse but then overlooks God's presence and power to overcome those sorrows can easily become depressed. The absence of God in her thinking leads to the sorrowing without hope that is depression. Biblical counselor Wayne Mack describes the outcome: "Depression is caused by a person's response to an event in their life, not the event itself."[7]

In cases of depression in adult survivors, an unbiblical response to suffering is what some victims have chosen for themselves, and it is something that can be resolved on the heart level with confession and repentance as they choose to think God's truth (1 John 1:9). Submission to these truths requires behavioral change as well, since wrong responses are to be replaced with obedient ones.[8] This process transforms desires, thinking, and behavior in depressed women as they put off their fleshly responses and intentionally follow Christ's command in "not returning evil for evil or insult for insult" (1 Peter 3:9a).

The abused child, who is tempted to respond with hopelessness and despair resulting in overwhelming feelings of depression, can recognize

---

[7] Wayne Mack, *Out of the Blues: Dealing with the Blues of Depression & Loneliness* (Bemidji, MN: Focus Publishing, Inc., 2006), 47.

[8] Ibid., 63-65.

that hope placed in God alone will never be lost. The counselor who teaches a child this truth is laying a foundation that prevents the hopelessness that leads to depression (Psalm 62:5-8).

Guilt and Shame

Guilt and shame are two responses that are closely linked. "The Bible uses many emotionally charged words to describe shame: reproach, dishonor, humiliation, and disgrace."[9] Each of these words and images are ones to which child sexual abuse victims can relate. In dealing with shame, Christ's death becomes a powerful way of escape for suffering women, for He has experienced the depth of shame that allows Him to be a sympathetic Savior (Hebrews 4:14-16). By this death, He has overcome the power of the sinner who violated these women as children, and if they are believers, they share in His victory.[10]

Knowing these truths brings healing to suffering children and adults who may feel isolated, believing that no one truly understands them. Once

---

[9] Justin S. Holcomb and Lindsey A. Holcomb, *Rid of My Disgrace: Hope and Healing for Victims of Sexual Assault*, (Wheaton, IL: Crossway, 2011), 91.

[10] Ibid., 99-100.

they understand Christ's suffering on their behalf, spiritual intimacy with God can become a reality.

Another long-term effect of child sexual abuse may be guilt. Guilt is a biblical term that describes a woman's "culpability before a holy God."[11] For survivors of child sexual abuse, guilt can be complicated since victims often take responsibility for their offender's sins.[12] Elyse Fitzpatrick writes, "It is easier to believe they did something that caused the abuse rather than believing the person they loved and trusted was wicked."[13]

In these cases, a victim's sense of guilt is unjustified. If, however, a victim is convicted that he or she has sinned in some way and is bearing genuine guilt as a result of that sin, 1 John 1:9 provides the remedy: "If we confess our sins, He is faithful and righteous to forgive us our sins and to cleanse us from all unrighteousness."

If abused children are feeling guilty, the counselor must lovingly investigate any reason for these feelings. If a child has sinned in response

---

[11] Elyse Fitzpatrick, "Counseling Women Abused as Children," *Women Helping Women,* ed. Elyse Fitzpatrick, 339-66 (Eugene, OR: Harvest House Publishers, 1997), 357.

[12] Ibid., 356.

[13] Ibid.

to abuse, he or she can resolve that guilt and shame through confession.

Every abused child can be comforted with the truth that much of the shame and guilt he or she is experiencing rightly belongs to the abuser. Re-assigning guilt and shame where it belongs is a key task in counseling sexually abused children.

Anger, Unforgiveness, and Bitterness

Anger, unforgiveness, and bitterness are related to each other. Though anger is a righteous re-sponse to the evil of child sexual abuse, many abused children have sinned in their anger by refusing to forgive their abuser.[14] This anger and

---

[14] We realize that it is not up to us to take revenge on others who have wronged us, or even to want to do so, because God has reserved that right for Himself. "Beloved, never avenge yourselves, but leave it to the wrath of God, for it is written, 'Vengeance is mine, I will repay, says the Lord'" (Romans 12:19). In this way whenever we have been wronged, we can give into God's hands any desire to harm or pay back the person who has wronged us, know-ing that every wrong in the universe will ultimately be paid for—either it will turn out to have been paid for by Christ when He died on the cross (if the wrongdoer becomes a Christian), or it will be paid for at the final judgment (for those who do not trust in Christ for salvation). But in either case we can give the situation into God's hands, and then pray that the wrongdoer will trust Christ for salvation and thereby receive forgiveness of his or her sins. "This thought should keep us from harboring bitterness or resentment in our hearts for injustices we have suffered that have not been made right: God is just, and we can leave these situations in his hands, knowing that he will

unforgiveness breeds bitterness that expresses itself in a desire for revenge.[15] God's prescribed response to anger, unforgiveness, and bitterness is forgiveness. It was modeled by Christ on the cross as He said, "Father, forgive them; for they do not know what they are doing" (Luke 23:34); and it was commanded by Him when He said this to His followers: "I say to you, love your enemies and pray for those who persecute you" (Matthew 5:44). An obedient response, no matter how difficult the situation, recognizes God's right to judge and punish sin (Romans 12:19).[16] The counselor and counselee must recognize that forgiveness does not mean reconciliation and the restoration of the relationship, because apart from repentance and transformation in the life of the abuser, there is no basis for relationship and the danger posed by the abuser still remains.

Children are able to forgive their abusers by following Christ's example. The truths from 1 Corinthians 5:12-13 and Romans 12:19 help

---

someday right all wrongs and give absolutely fair rewards and punishments." Wayne Grudem, *Systematic Theology: An Introduction to Biblical Doctrine* (Grand Rapids, MI: Zondervan, 2000), 1147-1148.

[15] Holcomb and Holcomb, *Rid of My Disgrace*, 126.

[16] See Wayne A. Grudem, *Systematic Theology: An Introduction to Biblical Doctrine* (Grand Rapids, MI: Intervarsity Press, 1994) for an in-depth explanation of these doctrines.

them to understand that the abuser is under God's judgment rather than theirs.

Distrust

Distrust that hinders interpersonal relation-ships is another commonly identified response to child sexual abuse. It characterizes human relationships but also describes a survivor's thoughts about God. In the human mind, God is no longer trustworthy because He did not step in and stop the abuse.[17] Choosing the biblical perspective found in Romans 8:28-29 not only reminds believers of God's power to use all things for their good, but also confirms that conformity to the image of Christ is His re-demptive plan for this suffering.

Distrust impacts human relationships as well. Many victims of child sexual abuse will exhibit extreme passivity and people-pleasing behavior so that they can protect themselves from hurt.[18] In order to experience healthy relationships,

---

[17] Diane Mandt Langberg, *On the Threshold of Hope: Opening the Door to Healing for Survivors of Sexual Abuse* (Carol Stream, IL: Tyndale House Publishers, 1999), 91. As a longtime practitioner in the field of sexual abuse counseling, Langberg's experience provides her with the expertise necessary for the accurate description of abuse victims and their typical responses to abuse.

[18] Ibid., 171.

victims of child sexual abuse must be willing to relate to others.[19] The church provides the perfect environment in which these relationships can be established since God designed His church to be a family (1 John 3:1-2), and relationships are the foremost way He builds this family (Matthew 22:37-40).

Abused children are comforted as they focus on God and His character. As meditation on Him replaces meditation on their abuse, they will be spared a distrust of God that is destructive (Jeremiah 17:5-6). This redirection is a priority for the counselor who deals with sexually abused children.

Self-Harm

Self-destructive behaviors associated with child sexual abuse may include the following:

> Addictions to alcohol, food, spending, drugs, and sex are prevalent. These addictive behaviors are often used to comfort and self-soothe whenever the survivor is overwhelmed by anxiety or other painful feelings. Suicidal ideation and/or attempts may be recurring. Self-mutilation, a behavior that causes the survivor

---

[19] Ibid., 169.

extreme shame, is common. Burning, cutting, self-bruising, biting, sticking oneself with pins, scratching, and beating oneself about the head is common.[20]

Knowing and believing that true comfort can be found only in God is the key to redirecting those who have been abused away from these behaviors.[21] Truths that, when believed, have the power to transform these behaviors focus on God as the Comforter (John 14:26; 15:26). Turning away from self-destructive habits and to God is a new habit that must be practiced and acquired through a yielding of the will, yet these victims of child sexual abuse are not alone in their efforts, for the power of God working in them will produce not only the desire but also the ability to do what pleases Him (Philippians 2:13).

Children who self-harm may be seeking to atone for their sins by shedding their own blood or wounding their own bodies. If they have withdrawn their trust from God, they may try to save themselves by punishing themselves. The counselor can comfort them with the truth that Christ has already been punished for them so that they do not need to harm themselves (Isaiah 53:5-8)

[20] Diane Mandt Langberg, *Counseling Survivors of Sexual Abuse* (Maitland, FL: Xulon Press, 2003), 89.

[21] Ibid.

Attempts to escape the pain of the abuse through drugs and alcohol can be replaced with an escape to Jesus Himself (1 Corinthians 10:13). The other things are cheap and destructive substitutes for Him.

Sexual Problems

The final long-term side effect of child sexual abuse that will be addressed here is that of sexual difficulties. Scripture clearly teaches that God's design for sex in marriage is to reflect the intimacy and oneness that portrays His desire for a deep and intimate relationship with His people (Ephesians 5:30-32).[22] The sexual abuse of a child perverts God's design and, without the corrective of God's truth, can result in deceived thinking even into adulthood.

Survivors of child sexual abuse may believe that they are worthless objects because their bodies were used for another's pleasure without any regard for their needs and desires.[23] Deceptive thoughts and feelings can then produce promiscuous behavior or create sexual difficul-

---

[22] Daniel R. Heimbach, *True Sexual Morality: Recovering Biblical Standards for a Culture in Crisis* (Wheaton, IL: Crossway Books, 2004), 149.

[23] Holcomb and Holcomb, *Rid of My Disgrace*, 71.

ties in marriage.[24] Yet this kind of thinking does not reflect biblical truth.

Scripture makes clear that the worth of human beings comes not from how others have treated them, but from the fact that God has created them in His image.[25] In order for their sexual behavior to reflect this truth, the thoughts and hearts of these abused children must be transformed.

Jay Adams describes this process of transformation clearly: "Substantial change requires the Holy Spirit's alteration of the heart (one's inner life known only to God and oneself). Outward changes of any significance must begin there."[26] So even when child abuse is sexual, the remedy is dependent upon God's Word as the means by which He brings healing and change in the hearts of women and children.

Addressing sexual issues with children can be difficult. Asking the child open-ended ques-

---

[24] Fitzpatrick, "Counseling Women Abused as Children," 364.

[25] Raymond C. Ortlund, Jr., "Male-Female Equality and Male Headship: Genesis 1-3" in *Recovering Biblical Manhood and Womanhood: A Response to Evangelical Feminism*, eds. John Piper and Wayne Grudem (Wheaton, IL: Crossway Books, 2006), 100.

[26] Jay E. Adams, *How to Help People Change: The Four-Step Biblical Process* (Grand Rapid, MI: Ministry Resources Library of Zondervan Publishing House, 1986), xii.

tions to draw out unbiblical thinking is important. Teaching these children about God's design for sexual intimacy in simple terms is an important part of replacing any unbiblical thinking with biblical truth.

The counselor should also equip parents to teach these truths to their children so that the temptation to draw the wrong conclusions about God's design for sex can be corrected whenever necessary.

God's Truth and Responses in Abused Children

If you are working with a child who has been sexually abused and their parents are believers, encourage the parents to participate in helping their child think through these weighty matters. Give the parents specific tips and direction on how to approach conversations with their child, such as:

- Use questions to reveal your child's thoughts and feelings and encourage open communication. No question is off limits and none should be rebuked.

- Teach your child that this is family talk. It is fine to speak about this topic at home or to the police, but it is private and not something others need to know about.

- Answer your child's questions with Scripture to show what God says about his or her thoughts and feelings. Trust God to work through His Word (John 17:17).

- Don't feel like you have to give answers immediately. Take time to go away and pray and hear from the Lord and then respond. Let your child know that is what you are doing. This will cause him or her to trust in God for answers just like you do.

- Be aware that sexual abuse is a crisis to which a child will respond in one of two ways: either with rebellion or with trust in God.

How does the rebellious child react?

- Reinterpreting God's character in light of the event as he or she is tempted to doubt God's love and power.
- Responding to God and others with mistrust.
- Rejecting God because of the abuse.

How does the child who trusts God respond?

- Turning to God in the crisis.
- Trusting that God can answer

hard questions.
- Willing to believe that God will bring good out of evil.

As sexual abuse uncovers a child's heart, the parent plays a vital role in directing him or her toward God's truth so he or she can respond to God appropriately. Encouraging the child with Scripture will provide answers and prevent deception by Satan (John 8:44).

Truths that must be repeatedly emphasized include the following:

The Nature of God

He loves you.

> "For God is love." (1 John 4:8b)

> "For I am convinced that neither death, nor life, nor angels, nor principalities, nor things present, nor things to come, nor powers, nor height, nor depth, nor any other created thing, will be able to separate us from the love of God, which is in Christ Jesus our Lord." (Romans 8:38-39)

He is so powerful that nothing is too difficult for Him.

> "Ah Lord God! Behold, You have made the heavens and the earth by Your great power and by Your outstretched arm! Nothing is too difficult for You." (Jeremiah 32:17)

> "For nothing will be impossible with God." (Luke 1:37)

If you are sad, God cares. You can trust Him.

> "He heals the brokenhearted and binds up their wounds." (Psalm 147:3)

> "Trust in Him at all times, O people; pour out your heart before Him; God is a refuge for us." (Psalm 62:8)

When you wonder why, remember that God takes evil and uses it for good.

> "And we know that God causes all things to work together for good to those who love God, to those who are called according to His purpose." (Romans 8:28)

God knows your abuser mistreated you and does not blame you. In fact, God will punish this man or woman's sin.

> "And whoever receives one such child in My name receives Me; but whoever causes one of these little ones who believe in Me to stumble, it would be better for him to have a heavy millstone hung around his neck, and to be drowned in the depth of the sea." (Matthew 18:5-6)

> "Never take your own revenge, beloved, but leave room for the wrath of God, for it is written, 'Vengeance is Mine, I will repay,' says the Lord." (Romans 12:19)

Obedience to God

You can still believe in and obey God. When you do this, evil is defeated.

> "Do not be overcome by evil, but overcome evil with good." (Romans 12:21)

You can love your enemy and pray for him.

> "But I say to you, love your enemies and pray for those who persecute you." (Matthew 5:44)

You can forgive your enemy.

> "Whenever you stand praying, forgive, if you have anything against anyone, so that your Father who is in heaven will also forgive you your transgressions." (Mark 11:25)

While you are to love and forgive, this relationship is broken because of your abuser's sin. You cannot make him change—that is God's work. Since he has chosen to do evil, you must stay away from him.

> "My son, if sinners entice you, do not consent.… My son, do not walk in the way with them. Keep your foot from their path." (Proverbs 1:10, 15)

A Permanent Resolution

Resolving the problems associated with child sexual abuse, whether they are the immediate ones in childhood or the long-term ones in adulthood, is all dependent on a relationship with Jesus Christ and a knowledge of His Word. The abused child desperately needs the outside intervention of a Savior who can remove not only the stain of his or her own sin but also the stigma of victimization by an abuser. The surviving adult needs the comfort of truth that only God can give. For both the child and the adult, the only solution is the good news of Jesus Christ.

The Good News of Jesus Christ

Share with your counselee the good news of Jesus Christ. See a sample below of how to do so.

God tells us that He made us for Himself.

> "For by Him all things were created, both in the heavens and on earth, visible and invisible, whether thrones or dominions or rulers or authorities—*all things have been created through Him and for Him*." (Colossians 1:16)[27]

God tells us that all are separated from Him by our sin and that our sin will destroy us.

---

[27] Emphasis added for this Bible verse and all following verses.

> "For *all have sinned* and fall short of the glory of God." (Romans 3:23)

> "For the *wages of sin is death*, but the *free gift of God is eternal life* in Christ Jesus our Lord." (Romans 6:23)

This verse portrays two spiritual kingdoms. The kingdom into which we are born is characterized by sin, and as long as we remain in this kingdom, we are earning what we deserve—wages that pay out in death.

Yet God offers us the choice of another kingdom and another kind of life where He rules and freely extends the gift of a never-ending relationship with Himself—something we do not deserve.

As we make this decision about the kingdom in which we will live, we need to understand the character of the king of each kingdom.

The first kingdom is ruled by Satan, and John 8:44 describes his nature:

> "He was *a murderer* from the beginning, and does not stand in the truth because there is no truth in him. Whenever he

speaks a lie, he speaks from his own nature, for *he is a liar and the father of lies.*" (John 8:44b)

The second kingdom is ruled by Jesus Christ, who loves us and gives Himself for us.

> "For *Christ also died for sins* once for all, *the just for the unjust*, so that He might bring us to God, having been put to death in the flesh, but made alive in the spirit." (1 Peter 3:18)

In the first kingdom, the king deceives us so that he can kill us. In the second kingdom, the king loves us and dies for us so we can be saved from this destruction. Which kingdom will you choose?

In order to leave the kingdom of deception and death, there are several responses to God that we must make.

> We must agree with God that we have sinned—"For *all have sinned* and fall short of the glory of God." (Romans 3:23)

> We must believe that Jesus died in our place, taking the punishment we de-

serve—"For God so loved the world that *He gave His only begotten Son*, that whoever believes in Him shall not perish, but have eternal life." (John 3:16)

We must give ourselves completely to God—"If you confess with your mouth Jesus as Lord, and believe in your heart that God raised Him from the dead, you will be saved; for *with the heart a person believes, resulting in righteousness, and with the mouth he confesses, resulting in salvation.*" (Romans 10:9-10)

Will you make this choice right now?

If so, please take a moment to talk to God about this decision and know that what He has promised He will do. In the moment of this decision, He has moved you from one kingdom to another, and the rest of your life will be different because you have believed these life-changing truths.

PART OF THE BIBLICAL SOLUTIONS SERIES

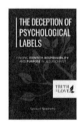

More Coming Soon

Biblical Solutions for the Problems People Face

The Association of Certified Biblical Counselors is committed to championing the sufficiency of Scripture for the Church as she engages the problems people face, speaking the truth in love. Christians have the responsibility to bring the truth of God to bear on the problems of everyday life, and to embody that truth in a life of love.

At ACBC, we seek to strengthen the Church to speak the truth in love by providing a quality training and certification process, a global network of like-minded individuals and institutions, and a source of practical and biblical resources for the Church.

In short, we seek to bring *biblical solutions for the problems people face*, upholding that the method God has given to do this is *truth in love*.

Find all our ACBC resources at www.biblicalcounseling.com.